A Cultural Affair

Visit www.booksurge.com to order additional copies.

A Cultural Affair
(A Book of Poems)

My Journey to My Gullah/Geechee People

Elder Carlie Towne

Acknowledgements

Tanki Gawd!

Special thanks to family and friends who encouraged me: Maudestine Martin, Elder Halim Abdul-Karim, Queen Quet Chieftess of the Gullah/Geechee Nation, Dr. George Brown, Elder Lisa Wineglass Small, Trent Walker, and my "sister circle," and Pauletta Hutchett.

A Cultural Affair

Cultural affair is about a young lady,
Who works in the corporate world.
She's actually a wanna' be.
She wanna be cultural, but . . . ,

She can't really be cultural,
ecause she's afraid what her friends might think
of her,
f she goes to work with her bangles on her arm,
And her cowrie shells on her anklet.

o, she just imagines that she put these things on.
And when she gets to work,
She sits in front of her computer,
And then she goes into Cyberspace.

Mud Cloth From Africa

Mud cloth from Africa,
Lively up my clothes,
An earring pierced in my nose.
Silver bangles on my arm,
On my anklet a cowrie charm.
Dreadlocks in my hair,
Now I'm all dolled up,
To go to a Cultural Affair.
Where? Right here,
Time? Anytime,
Place? Cyberspace.

You Got to Come to Charleston

When I would travel around the world,
Or well, not really around the world,
On the islands, in the Caribbean islands.
Especially people ask me where I was from.
I would say, "Charleston,"
And, I would always tell them,
You got to come to Charleston.
Charleston nice.
Then, I would tell them about all the beautiful
things we had,
Like you know, the Rainbow Row,
And the different little streets, cobblestone streets.
And I was so excited,
And I would especially tell them about the Gullah/
Geechee people there,
And the people who were so,
They seemed to be "cousins" to the people in the
islands.
I felt that I needed to let everyone know that,
Charleston is nice,
And that's just how I feel,
I feel like Charleston's nice.

Charleston Nice

Charleston nice,
Houses one room wide with piazza to the side,
Charleston nice,
Houses one room wide with piazza to the side,
Charleston nice,
Churches, St. Michael's and St. Philip's with steeple,
Charleston nice,
Gullah/Geechee spoken by both black and white
people,
Charleston nice,
Red rice and fish, a Charleston dish,
Charleston nice,
MOJA and Spoleto, you don't want to miss,
Charleston nice,
Come on sisters and brothers, and check out this,
Charleston nice,
Come to Charleston, enjoy the Gullah/Geechee life,
Charleston nice.

(Rap)
Red rice and fish,
And I'm guaranteed to make you smack your lips,
We also have our Charleston low country red rice dish,
Guaranteed to put that extra groove in your move,
With just a little wiggle in your giggle.

Ambassador for Charleston

I feel like I'm the Ambassador for Charleston,
Especially for the Gullah/Geechee people,
I cause they have a culture here that's really wonderful,
And it's still in tact,
And I want **all** the whole world to know about it.

So that's why I'd like to just call all the great women,
Like Terry McMillan and Maya Angelou and Oprah
Winfrey,
I want to say, "Y'all, Come on down,
Come on down to Carlie Towne."

So we can look at all the beautiful sites we have here,
Especially the beautiful houses.
It's just wonderful,
It's enchanting, I love it,
And I want everybody else to come see it.

Charleston is a Beautiful Place

Charleston is a beautiful place,
Full of charm and grace,
With different architectural forms,
You'll find Greek revival to Romanesque dome.

Row houses on the east side,
On the Battery, a Victorian house facing the tide,
On King Street, a Georgian house with chavote de
freeze,
British stayed there when Charleston was seized.

Cupola atop many houses sit,
Just as common in Charleston as shrimp and grits,
Our ancestors they had good taste,
They left Charleston with such architectural beauty
and grace.

(Rap of the Tour)
When I get to Charleston, I'll park my car,
Visiting the four corners of the law,
Where our City Hall is located,
Our market area, our museum, and Avery Research
Center.

Culture is Alive

The culture is alive here in Charleston,
And it's alive in basket making.

Ƴou can come to Charleston and you'll see these
ladies,
In the market area weaving their baskets.

It's amazing seeing these ladies doin' art,
That's hundreds and hundreds of years old.

It's like nostalgia.

Basket Weaving

Basket weaving is still alive,
Come to Africa from Sierra Leone tribes.

An ancient art brought from slave to Charleston's shore,
Now sold in the slave market and in the store.

See the magic of basket making,
Hear the story of how from generation to
generation the art's been taken.

Be sure to get a basket made of sweetgrass,
For you will capture Charleston present as well as
Africa's past.

The Angel Oak Tree

The majestic angel oak tree,
It tells a story of runaway slaves and how they
became free.

I is a thousand years old,
Many African stories I've heard told.

ve heard the chants of runaway slaves who cried
late at night,
ve heard a child say, "Mama, Mama, is the Masse
gonna' get us?"
N , young 'un, we gonna' stay right under the angel
oak tree,
Cause we gonna be free.

I've heard the chirps of beautiful birds,
That made music to poor Africans in flight,
I've heard Cato, a runaway slave say,
" efore I be a slave, I be buried under a stone in my
grave."

Look, listen my children, and you too will see,
I ow I, the majestic angel oak tree can talk to thee,
About how slaves of long time ago became free.

B ckground of this poem: *The Angel Oak Tree* is a
v y, very old tree, and it's in Johns Island. It's a very
n sterious tree that I have great love for because I

felt that a lot of our ancestors had to run there for shelter and that's why I wrote the poem in 1984. In 1996, I added some lines to it. It's one of those poems that touch the heart and the soul of every person that listens to it, because the tree actually talks to the audience.

Gullah/Geechee Nation

When visitors come to the Gullah/Geechee Nation,
They always come looking for the Gullah/Geechee
people.
Well, I be Gullah/Geechee, she be Gullah/
Geechee, they be Gullah/Geechee,
Gullah/Geechee all around you,
We be one big Gullah/Geechee family!

Carlie Towne in Gullah/Geechee Land

Carlie Towne in Gullah/Geechee land,
With 20 other Gullah/Geechee man,

Coming together in the hood,
Wishing to be understood.

Just like the Gullah/Geechee people and the rest,
Working together for success.

Acting like kings and queens,
Spreading the word about brothers and sisters in
the Caribbean.

Putting Gullah/Geechee culture on the map,
Doin' nothing but positive rap.

Ca eady baby,
Bun e toe,
Gullah, Gullah, Gullah!

Carlie Towne

Guess what?
It's springtime in Carlie Towne.
Bright misty morning, sun shining, flowers
blooming,
As a cool breeze blows gently through my window
pane,
Cowrie shell earrings dangling,
From the ears of a lovely Charleston Gullah/
Geechee girl,
As she moves her nod from side to side,
Seems to say to me,
"It's springtime and the sap is rising,
Watch out, Boy."

Background about this poem: *Carlie Towne* is a gift
from a friend or is a close relative. It's about a girl
that's flirting with this man, and he sees her, and
she says to her some cute stuff. She knows that he
really likes her. So, she says something real cute, real
southernly-like, real Charleston-like, real Gullah/
Geechee-like. And, I think that girl is really how I
can be sometimes.

Rap Sister Rap

Went to church tow Sundays ago,
Fell in love with Sister Moore,
She was praying and thankin' the Lord,
Up jumps Sister Louella,
She leap into the sky,
Started to rap about Jesus on high.
She says, *Breeze-a,*
Blowing through the trees-a,
Make me know a Jesus,
Only One could please us,
Thenk You, Thenk You, Jesus.

I wondered to myself,
How could she remember all the things to say,
The rhythm and the cliché,
I could not believe all the rap I had heard,
And the sister was sayin' it word for word.

After church, I asked her:
How you know to rap so well?
She said, "Inside of me an inner voice dwells,
She said, It was the Holy Spirit and the way she
rapped, it was inherent,

So rapping is nothing new,
First time I heard it was in 1952.
It was Sister Louella,
Rappin' in the pew.
Rap Sister, Rap Sister.

Oh, Jesus, Oh Jesus,
Talkin' Bout Jesus,
I'm Talkin' Bout Jesus.

Background about this poem: *Rap Sister Rap*, I think, is the religious part of me coming out. The first time, I saw my first rap concert was in the Church. It was Sister Louella, and she was rappin'. She was up in the pew and she was doin' her thing, and it was positive too. And she was talking about Jesus and I enjoyed every minute of it. I can still remember it; five years old, sitting there looking at this lady, and she was just going on and on. I said to myself, "Gee, she can rap."

Union Hike

Barbara and Marian, Afro Dan,
Bertha Ann, Bootsie, and Big Sam,
Fried chicken, collard green, sweet potato pie,
Fish fryin,' Isabella Joint of course, July,
People, places, and food,
All of these livin' in Union Hike hood.

Background about this poem: *Union Hike* is where
my roots are. It's where my journey began. It's where
Isabella Joint was on the corner of Groveland and
Buchanan, where we used to go and hear, "Long Tall
Sally Duck Him In The Alley." I just have to talk about
it because so many good things happened here.

Shrimp & Gravy

The night I met my husband to be,
Who at that time was in the Navy.
I had invited him over to my house,
For some shrimp and gravy.

I sauteed them shrimp until they turned pink,
Then I got me a big pot from under the sink.
I washed some long grain rice, got the knife out,
And the onion, then I began to slice.

I threw them onion in the pot with the shrimp,
I let them onion cook until they became real limp.
I put a big pot of rice on the stove big eye,
Then went and sat next to my Navy guy.

We talked about what he liked to eat,
I must have ESP, because shrimp was his favorite treat.
After he tasted my shrimp, gravy and rice,
He told me he thought Charleston girls were very
nice.

Well, the rest is history,
Because the next thing he told me was that he
wanted me to be his wife.
Guys, marry a Charleston woman and eat shrimp,
gravy and rice,
For the rest of your life.

Background about this poem: *Shrimp & Gravy* is one of my favorite dishes, that's why I wrote about it. Before I became a vegetarian, I used to eat shrimp and gravy all the time. The Navy part came into the poem because I lived in a neighborhood in Union Hike where there were a bunch of Navy guys. All over the place were these Navy guys. If you didn't marry a Navy guy, well, you didn't get married. So, when I thought about this story, I said, "Yeah, Shrimp, Gravy, and a Navy." Yeah, that's just how I wrote it.

Shirley Mae and Me

It was Shelly Mae and me,
And Mrs. Fulfoot invited us to her porch for tea.
She was a big strapped Gullah/Geechee ooman,
With a cane she walked,
It was about the future she'd talk.

She'd say, look down and you'll always see,
All those people trying to get into heaven.
We didn't really understand this old lady because,
Shelly Mae and me,
We were only seven.

Peaches she would give us,
And we would listen to her prophecies until dusk.
Some say she was supposed to be a hag,
That could be true, because when she walked,
Her left foot she would drag.

Last time we sat with Mrs. Fulfoot she looked down,
As she looked, up danced a roach.
Still she continued to stare on the floor,
Then all of a sudden she got up,
And started to walk in the living room door.

Shelly Mae and me,
Didn't know what she was going to do.
But we followed her in the living room to the
kitchen all the way through.
She dragged her left foot,
As she passed the black stove with soot.

Shelly Mae and me began to shake,
I remember Shelly Mae saying, "Don't let Mrs.
Fulfoot root us,
For heaven's sake."
Finally, Mrs. Fulfoot flung open the kitchen door,
Shelly Mae and me, ran out like lions in an uproar.

As fast as a thief in the night,
Shelly Mae and me didn't look back,
Until Mrs. Fulfoot's house was out of sight.
The next day we met at the Chinaberry tree space,
Shelly Mae asked me if I wanted to go to Mrs.
Fulfoot place.

I said sure, why not,
As a rock on the ground made my bare feet hot.
After all, she had some good peaches,
She would let them sit in the sun
Until they almost rot.

But what else could two fast Gullah/Geechee girls,
Do on a steaming hot day?
A neighbor man's voice at a distance says:
"You ain't had no business over there no way."

Background about this poem: I remember writing *Shirley Mae and Me* because it's a story about two Gullah/Geechee girls, and one of the girls was a friend of mine who I had been in school with a long time. We used to sit on Mrs. Fulfoot's porch. Mrs. Fulfoot was an older Gullah/Geechee ooman who would give us peaches, and we would enjoy listening to her old stories—stories of long ago. I wanted to relate that to the kids of today, because very seldom do they get a chance to talk to a lot of the older people. It was such a wonderful story that "danced in my head" forever, so I wanted the kids to know about it. That's why I wrote it.

Charleston Place

Charleston, South Carolina is the place to be,
The city by the sea,
With tons of places and people,
And things to see.

Look, sweetgrass baskets,
Iron gates,
Cobblestone streets,
Single houses.

Mr. Philip Simmons the Ironsmith,
Mrs. Sunshine the Flower Lady,
Elder Halim the Jewelry Artist,
Ché the Poet.

Spanish moss and azaleas,
Carriage rides,
And of course,
Lots and lots of tour guides.

Background about this poem: Emmanuel AME Church, Meeting Street, The Battery, the market area; all these places helped me write my poem, *Charleston A Place.* In fact, after I thought about it, maybe I should have said, *Charleston The Place.*

We Be A Gullah/Geechee Family

We are a Gullah/Geechee family,
My husband and me and baby make three.
Spreading the word about the Gullah/Geechee Nation,
And where the Gullah/Geechee be.

It be right here,
From Cape Fear, North Carolina to Jacksonville,
Florida, and 30 miles inland.
So come and listen to our shouts and rhyme,
Gullah/Geechee has changed a little bit at a time.

In the Gullah/Geechee Nation the language can
be found,
But most of the time it's coded with a more
marketable sound.
Nowaday it's about the way we talk,
Gullah/Geechee be about the way we dance, sing,
shout, and walk.

We still shout about who we are,
About what we sell.
About who is saved,
And who is going to hell.

Come on, shout along with me,
"Shak steak, Shak steak.
En need no graby,
Mek e o graby.
Tye Dye, Tye Dye, Tye Dye, Tye Dye.

About the Author

Elder Carlie Towne, a native of Charleston, SC, studied Cultural Anthropology at the College of Charleston. It is her constant travel abroad that has influenced her to compose such a brilliant work. Elder Carlie Towne is also the Director of the Gullah/Geechee Angel Network and the Minister of Information for the Gullah/Geechee Nation under the leadership of Queen Quet Chieftess of the Gullah/Geechee Nation.

Elder Carlie's poetry has been manifested by the life experiences of the people of the Carolina Sea islands. A Cultural Affair is the first of a collection of Elder Towne's anthology depicting Gullah/Geechee life. Through her words, the life and times of Charleston's rich ethnicity are expressed. The first of its kind in the 'low country,' A Cultural Affair features a combination of poems and literary cameo appearances of figures in the Charleston area.

Her words are much more than random stanzas put together for rhyming. These words are expressions of the author's soul. To learn of the importance of the Gullah/Geechee Nation's contribution to America, one merely has to relax, kick one's shoes off, and enjoy. Remember . . . it's A Cultural Affair.

To have this book sent to your address, please contact Elder Carlie Towne by email at ctowne@gullahgeecheeangelnetwork.com or by telephone at (843) 572-6788. Please visit our web site at www.gullahgeecheeangelnetwork.com.

Made in the USA
Columbia, SC
09 February 2024